GORSE FIRES

GORSE FIRES

MICHAEL LONGLEY

Secker & Warburg
POETRY

First published in Great Britain 1991 by
Martin Secker & Warburg Limited
Michelin House, 81 Fulham Road,
London SW3 6RB

Reprinted 1991

A CIP catalogue record for this book
is available from the British Library

ISBN 0 436 25674 6

Printed in Great Britain by
St Edmundsbury Press Limited, Bury St Edmunds, Suffolk

Between now and one week ago when the snow fell, a bird landed
Where they lie, and made cosier and whiter the white patchwork:
And where I imagine her ashes settling on to his collarbone,
The tracks vanish between wing-tips symmetrically printed.

CONTENTS

ACKNOWLEDGEMENTS

Acknowledgements are due to the following:

BBC, *Belfast Newsletter, Gown, Honest Ulsterman, Irish Literary Supplement, Irish Times, Krino, Lines, London Review of Books, Maryland Review, Massachusetts Review, New Statesman, North Dakota Review, Observer, Partisan Review, Poetry Book Society Bulletin, Poetry Ireland, Poetry Wales*, Radio Telefis Eireann, *Times Literary Supplement*

Section I of 'Ghetto' (under the title 'Belongings'), 'In a Mississauga Garden', 'Font' and 'Laertes' first appeared in the *New Yorker*.

'Jug Band' was written specially for *Philip Larkin: A Tribute*, edited by George Hartley (Marvell Press).

A British Airways Commonwealth Poetry Prize and awards from the Charitable Irish Society of Boston and the Irish American Cultural Institute were much appreciated.

Acknowledgement is also due to Anvil Press for permission to print as an epigraph a line from Paul Celan's 'Talglicht' in Michael Hamburger's translation.

Shells I speak and light clouds, and a boat buds in the rain.

PAUL CELAN

SEA SHANTY

I would have waited under the statue of Eros
While the wind whistled in my bell-bottoms,
Taken my bearings from the blink of daylight
Her thighs and feathery maidenhair let through.
But now from the high ground of Carrigskeewaun
I watch Lesbos rising among the islands.
Rain shivers off the machair, and exposes me
In my long-johns, who dozed on her breastbone,
On pillows of sea-pink beyond the shingle,
Who mumbled into the ringlets at her ear
My repertoire of sea shanties and love songs.
I shake like a rock-fern, and my ill will
And smoky breath seem to wither the lichens.
I am making do with what has been left me,
The saltier leaves of samphire for my salad.
At midnight the moon goes, then the Pleiades,
A sparkle of sand grains on my wellingtons.

PHOSPHORESCENCE

There was light without heat between the stepping stones
And the duach, at every stride the Milky Way.
Her four or five petals hanging from an eyelash,
Venus bloomed like brookweed next to the Pleiades.

INSOMNIA

I could find my way to either lake at this late hour
Sleepwalking after the night-alarms of whooper swans.
If I get to sleep, the otter I have been waiting for
Will surface in the estuary near the stepping stones.

WASHING

All the washing on the line adds up to me alone.
When the cows go home and the golden plover calls
I bring it in, but leave pegged out at intervals
Dooaghtry Lake and David's Lake and Corragaun,
Gaps in the dunes, a sky-space for the lapwings
And the invisible whiteness of your underthings.

MIGRATIONS

I have hidden a key under the dry-stone wall
For lovers to make after me a home from home –
My gifts turf in a creel, buckets of lake water,
Their witnesses waders gathering for Greenland,
The Arctic, and pebbly nests below the snow-line.
I sleep on the other side of the hill from them.

MADAME BUTTERFLY

Through atmospherics I hear you die again.
Death is white as your lover's uniform, as snow
When it covers the whiteness of almond petals.
Worse weather blows your papery house away.
Now I listen for the snow bunting's arrival,
A flute-note from crevices and rocky scree.

BETWEEN HOVERS

in memory of Joe O'Toole

And not even when we ran over the badger
Did he tell me he had cancer, Joe O'Toole
Who was psychic about carburettor and clutch
And knew a folk cure for the starter-engine.
Backing into the dark we floodlit each hair
Like a filament of light our lights had put out
Somewhere between Kinnadoohy and Thallabaun.
I dragged it by two gritty paws into the ditch.
Joe spotted a ruby where the canines touched.
His way of seeing me safely across the duach
Was to leave his porch light burning, its sparkle
Shifting from widgeon to teal on Corragaun Lake.
I missed his funeral. Close to the stony roads
He lies in Killeen Churchyard over the hill.
This morning on the burial mound at Templedoomore
Encircled by a spring tide and taking in
Cloonaghmanagh and Claggan and Carrigskeewaun,
The townlands he'd wandered tending cows and sheep,
I watched a dying otter gaze right through me
At the islands in Clew Bay, as though it were only
Between hovers and not too far from the holt.

OTTERS

I

As though it were the only one in Ireland
I lie above Corragaun and watch an otter
Tying and untying knots in the undertow
And wiring me like a harebell to the wind.

II

An upturned currach at Allaran Point
And a breaking wave are holt and hover
Until the otter, on wet sand in between,
Engraves its own reflection and departure.

DETOUR

I want my funeral to include this detour
Down the single street of a small market town,
On either side of the procession such names
As Philbin, O'Malley, MacNamara, Keane.
A reverent pause to let a herd of milkers pass
Will bring me face to face with grubby parsnips,
Cauliflowers that glitter after a sunshower,
Then hay rakes, broom handles, gas cylinders.
Reflected in the slow sequence of shop windows
I shall be part of the action when his wife
Draining the potatoes into a steamy sink
Calls to the butcher to get ready for dinner
And the publican descends to change a barrel.
From behind the one locked door for miles around
I shall prolong a detailed conversation
With the man in the concrete telephone kiosk
About where my funeral might be going next.

PURLIN

Where there's nothing to fell but hazel scrub and hawthorn
You will need to disinter the wood to make your purlin,
Deciphering the slow gasses that, for thousands of years,
Have cast from underground the shadow of a tree-trunk
By keeping the frost away that soon will come over you
After you fall asleep in the roof-space, timber's grave.

IN AILLWEE CAVE

There must be grazing overhead, hazel thickets,
Pavements the rain is dissolving, springs and graves,
Darkness above the darkness of the seepage of souls
And hedges where goosegrass spills its creamy stars.

PEREGRINE

I had been waiting for the peregrine falcon
As a way of coming to terms with the silence,
As a way of getting closer to you – an idea
Above the duach, downy whirlwinds, the wind's
Mother-of-pearl for instance, an eddy of bones.

Did the peregrine falcon when I was cycling
To meet you, swoop from the corner of my eye
And in and out of the culvert and out of sight
As though to avoid colliding with me – wings
Under the road, a blur of spokes and feathers?

GORSE FIRES

Cattle out of their byres are dungy still, lambs
Have stepped from last year as from an enclosure.
Five or six men stand gazing at a rusty tractor
Before carrying implements to separate fields.

I am travelling from one April to another.
It is the same train between the same embankments.
Gorse fires are smoking, but primroses burn
And celandines and white may and gorse flowers.

MERCURY

An inch above the horizon
Where the fields dip, Mercury
Seems to be reflecting Venus,
As though you were carrying
Through the gate a candle flame
And shielding it with your hand
For fear it might be put out
By the wind or the distance.

GOLDCREST

When you weighed against
A dried-out wine cork
The goldcrest, then buried
The twelfth of an ounce
Which was its eye, feathers
And inner workings,
Did you release, love,
Among the tree tops
The ghost of a bouquet?

REMEMBERING CARRIGSKEEWAUN

A wintry night, the hearth inhales
And the chimney becomes a windpipe
Fluffy with soot and thistledown,
A voice-box recalling animals:
The leveret come of age, snipe
At an angle, then the porpoises'
Demonstration of meaningless smiles.
Home is a hollow between the waves,
A clump of nettles, feathery winds,
And memory no longer than a day
When the animals come back to me
From the townland of Carrigskeewaun,
From a page lit by the Milky Way.

HOMECOMING

The brightest star came out, the day-star, dawn's star
And the seafaring ship drew near to Ithaca, to home
And that harbour named after the old man of the sea, two
Headlands huddling together as breakwater, windbreak,
Haven where complicated vessels float free of moorings
In their actual mooring-places.
                                    At the harbour-head
A long-leaved olive overshadows a shadowy cave
Full of bullauns, basins hollowed out of stone, stone
Jars for honey-bees, looms of stone on which are woven
Sea-purplish things – also, inextinguishable springs
And two ways in, one looking north where men descend
While the other faces south, a footpath for the gods.

When they had scrunched ashore at this familiar cove
And disembarked, they lifted Odysseus out of his hollow
Just as he was, linen sheet and glossy rug and all,
And put him to bed on the sand, still lost in sleep.

THE VELOCIPEDE

He walks past my bedroom window carrying a spade.
That Joseph Murphy, father of four sets of twins,
Jockey, lover of horses, the gun club's secretary,
Should hide in his cottage a ledger full of poems
Is hardly surprising: consider his grandfather
Who beachcombed from the strand barrels and spars
And built the first velocipede in Thallabaun.
Out of an umbrella and old sheets he improvised
A parachute, launched himself from the byre roof
And after a brief flight was taken to hospital.
On home-made crutches and slipping all the tethers
Joseph Murphy's grandfather swings past my window.

HALLEY'S COMET

Homage to Erik Satie

It was the seventeenth variation after all.
The original theme had fluttered out of my hands
And upside down on the linoleum suggested it.
An ink blot on the stave inspired the modulation,
Or was it a bloodstain, a teardrop's immortality
Perfectly pitched between parallels, horizontals,
The provisional shorelines, amphibian swamps?
I got drunk on a pint mug full of white feathers.
I couldn't sleep because inside my left nostril
A hair kept buzzing with signals from Halley's comet
As it swung its skirt of heavenly dust particles
On a parabola around the electric light bulb.
This won't recur for another seventy-six years.

JUG BAND

in memory of Philip Larkin

We would follow that New Orleans marching band
As it passes the settee for the hundredth time,
But we have left clarinet and drums behind
And make up the instruments, and then the theme,

And the theme is the making up of instruments,
Jugs and kazoos for us to improvise our souls,
Thimbles for keeping time with and making sense
On a washboard of our uncomplicated roles.

THE SHACK

for Dillon and Guinn

I lie awake between the two sleeping couples.
Their careful breathing in the Blue Ridge Mountains
Disturbs me more than the engine ticking over
At the end of the lane, the repetitive whippoorwill,
The downpour's crescendo on corrugated iron.
Though there are no doors between them and me, perhaps
They will risk making love like embarrassed parents
While I remain motionless on my creaking divan.
They have shown me a copperhead, indian fire pinks
And buzzards like mobiles where the storm clouds hang.
I might as well be outside in the steamy field
Interrupting again the opossums' courtship,
Paralysing with torchlight pink noses, naked tails
Just beyond the shithouse where, like a fall of snow,
The equalising lime has covered our excrement.
Tomorrow when we pass the Pentecostal church
The wayside pulpit will read 'Thanks, Lord, for the rain.'

HUMMING BIRD

When a single sheet's too heavy and the night perspires
And the wild turkey cock blunders from the undergrowth,
I long for fast wings in the branches, the hesitations
Among these unknown flowers of my first humming bird.

QUAILS' EGGS

We listen for quails among ferns and twigs
and translate that call as 'wet-my-lips'.
Food-gatherers, eaters of quails' eggs
We throw our voices like ventriloquists.

AN AMISH RUG

As if a one-room schoolhouse were all we knew
And our clothes were black, our underclothes black,
Marriage a horse and buggy going to church
And the children silhouettes in a snowy field,

I bring you this patchwork like a smallholding
Where I served as the hired boy behind the harrow,
Its threads the colour of cantaloupe and cherry
Securing hay bales, corn cobs, tobacco leaves.

You may hang it on the wall, a cathedral window,
Or lay it out on the floor beside our bed
So that whenever we undress for sleep or love
We shall step over it as over a flowerbed.

IN A MISSISSAUGA GARDEN

The ghosts of the aunt and uncles I never knew
Put in an appearance when I meet my cousin.
Charlie, big in the Union, straightens his plus-fours.
Hugh is curing home-grown tobacco in the garage
While my grandparents lie upstairs, out of sorts.
Seamstress to the Court, Daisy burns a cigarette hole
In the chesterfield, then makes the tea for everyone.
Maurice keeps fiddling with the wind-up gramophone.
Having come all the way across the Atlantic
From Clapham Common to this Mississauga garden,
They flit out of sight like the different robins
Or the blackbird with flashes of red on its wings.

SWALLOW

When the swallow detoured into the kitchen
Kissing corners, highlighting the dusty shelves
With its underside, those exhausted feathers
That never quite made it through the open door,
We too were on the verge of moving house:

In the fridge a neglected rainbow trout,
A mouse mummifying underneath the piano,
Dead friends, draughts from the rafters, artisans
From the Land of Promise or thereabouts
Thatching with the wings of birds our house.

THE HIP-BATH

My body has felt like a coalminer's black body
Folded into the hip-bath, a blink of white eyes
And then darkness, warm water coloured by darkness
And the hands that trickle down my dusty spine.

THE FIREPLACE

In the fireplace a pyramid of stones, soul-stones
Remembering the molten core, the Milky Way:
Balanced on top an eggshell full of rainwater
About to boil, if our bodies can get close enough.

AUBADE

after Nuala ní Dhomhnaill

It's all the same to morning what it dawns on –
On the bickering of jackdaws in leafy trees;
On that dandy from the wetlands, the green mallard's
Stylish glissando among reeds; on the moorhen
Whose white petticoat flickers around the boghole;
On the oystercatcher on tiptoe at low tide.

It's all the same to the sun what it rises on –
On the windows in houses in Georgian squares;
On bees swarming to blitz suburban gardens;
On young couples yawning in unison before
They do it again; on dew like sweat or tears
On lilies and roses; on your bare shoulders.

But it isn't all the same to us that night-time
Runs out; that we must make do with today's
Happenings, and stoop and somehow glue together
The silly little shards of our lives, so that
Our children can drink water from broken bowls,
Not from cupped hands. It isn't the same at all.

GLASS FLOWERS

I

I would bring glass flowers to the broken marriages
Because of their flowering time, the once and for all
Hard petals, cups and saucers from a doll's house,
The imaginary roots that grow into the table.

II

The glass iron cooling in your hand will double as
A darning last, a curve of light beneath the holes:
Let me rock along the seams with it before your
Breath condenses on heels and elbows made of glass.

TREE-HOUSE

When he described how he had built the ingenious bedroom
Around that bushy olive-tree – their sign and secret –
The stone-work tightly set, the thatching weatherproof,
Double-doors well-hinged; how he had lopped off branches
And with his adze smoothed down the trunk and got it plumb
– The beginnings of a bed, the bedpost – and with his auger
Drilled the frame, inlaying silver, ivory, gold; and then
How he had interwoven thongs of ox-hide, coloured purple –
She believed at last in the master-craftsman, Odysseus,
And tangled like a child in the imaginary branches
Of the tree-house he had built, love poet, carpenter.

COUCHETTE

With my wife, son, daughter in layers up the walls
This room on wheels has become the family vault.
They have fallen asleep, dreams stopping and starting
As my long coffin wobbles on the top couchette.
Shunted down a siding, we shall wait for centuries
Before hurtling to places we have never seen.
No more than a blink of light, a tinkle of bangles,
The old woman who joins us at Turin will leave
Crusts and a plastic bottle of mineral water.
Soon her space will be taken by a younger lady
We met four thousand years ago in Fiesole,
Her face still to be uncovered, and at her feet
A pet cat who has also been wrapped in bandages.

CATHEDRAL

I

Between the bells and prayers a flower-seller calls
Prices and flower-names the dome translates to echoes,
As though a pigeon had flapped in from the piazza
And perched on the chalice and sipped the sacrament.

II

Because it was dragged on a cart to the cathedral
By untamed calves, the wooden body has emerged
From candle-smoke and incense and, dressed up as God,
Moves through the market to locate those animals.

III

The puppy supposed to suggest a faithful wife
Has nearly nipped her toes for centuries, and begs
To be taken for a walk outside this building
Where stones eat flesh and moonlight eats the stones.

IL VOLTO SANTO

We've put a necklace on the naked wood, a crown,
A tunic embroidered with gold, expensive clothes.

Which one of us will fill a sponge with vinegar,
And hoist it upon hyssop, and give him to drink?

FONT

for Manus Carson

I

On its little island in the middle of the font
A lamb looks over its shoulder at the furore
Of what appear to be dolphins and porpoises
Leaping out of the holy water, but the details
Have been erased by ripples from priests' fingers
Moving like moorhens or geese or swans landing.

II

A pagan and one of those awkward Protestants
I still can imagine beneath the rose-window
A font for you and for my own son and daughters.
Prose is a river of words washing your name now
And poetry a fountain of vowels and consonants.
On your forehead all waters are holy waters.

THE MAN OF TWO SORROWS

Since the day after he was conceived his father
Was killed, he will become The Man of Two Sorrows
Whose mother is wading into the river to delay
His birth, squatting all night on a stepping stone
That flattens his head, headstone pressing fontanel,
Waters breaking under water that nearly drowns him,
Until the morning when he is born and she dies
And the drops of first milk vanish in the river.

EURYCLEIA

I

Eurycleia fetched a basin, poured cold water into it,
Added hot water, and got ready to wash his feet.
But Odysseus shifted out of the firelight, afraid
She might notice his scar, the key to his identity,
A wound a boar inflicted years back, a flesh-wound.
His wet-nurse cradled his foot in her hands and touched
The scar, and recognising him she let go of his leg
Which clattered into the basin – water everywhere,
Such pain and happiness, her eyes filling with tears,
Her old voice cracking as she stroked his beard and whispered
'You are my baby boy for sure and I didn't know you
Until I had fondled my master's body all over.'

II

I began like Odysseus by loving the wrong woman
Who has disappeared among the skyscrapers of New York
After wandering for thousands of years from Ithaca.
She alone remembers the coppice, dense and overgrown,
Where in a compost of dead leaves the boar conceals
Its bristling spine and fire-red eyes and white tusks.

NORTHERN LIGHTS

When you woke me up and showed me through the window
Curtains of silk, luminous smoke, ghost fires,
A convergence of rays above the Black Mountain,
The northern lights became our own magnetic field –
Your hand on my shoulder, your tobacco-y breath
And the solar wind that ruffled your thinning hair.

LAERTES

When he found Laertes alone on the tidy terrace, hoeing
Around a vine, disreputable in his gardening duds,
Patched and grubby, leather gaiters protecting his shins
Against brambles, gloves as well, and, to cap it all,
Sure sign of his deep depression, a goatskin duncher,
Odysseus sobbed in the shade of a pear-tree for his father
So old and pathetic that all he wanted then and there
Was to kiss him and hug him and blurt out the whole story,
But the whole story is one catalogue and then another,
So he waited for images from that formal garden,
Evidence of a childhood spent traipsing after his father
And asking for everything he saw, the thirteen pear-trees,
Ten apple-trees, forty fig-trees, the fifty rows of vines
Ripening at different times for a continuous supply,
Until Laertes recognised his son and, weak at the knees,
Dizzy, flung his arms around the neck of great Odysseus
Who drew the old man fainting to his breast and held him there
And cradled like driftwood the bones of his dwindling father.

THE BALLOON

You are a child in the dream and not my mother.
I float above your head as in a hot air balloon
That casts no shadow on you looking up at me
And smiling and waving and running without a limp
Across the shallow streams and fields of shiny grass
As though there were neither malformation nor pain.
This is the first time ever I have seen you running.
You are a child in the dream and not my mother
Which may be why I call out from the balloon to you:
'Jump over the hedges, Connie, jump over the trees.'

ANTICLEIA

If at a rock where the resonant rivers meet, Acheron,
Pyriphlegethon, Cocytus, tributary of the Styx, you dig
A pit, about a cubit each way, from knuckles to elbow,
And sacrifice a ram and a black ewe, bending their heads
Towards the outer darkness, while you face the water,
And so many souls of the anaemic dead come crowding in
That you hold them back with your bayonet from the blood
Only to recognise among the zombies your own mother,
And if, having given her blood to drink and talked about home,
You lunge forward three times to hug her and three times
Like a shadow or idea she vanishes through your arms
And you ask her why she keeps avoiding your touch and weep
Because here is your mother and even here in Hades
You could comfort each other in a shuddering embrace,
Will she explain that the sinews no longer bind her flesh
And bones, that the irresistible fire has demolished these,
That the soul takes flight like a dream and flutters in the sky,
That this is what happens to human beings when they die?

ICON

When I told you on the day my mother died
'I am an orphan now', you crouched over me
And protected me with your shoulders and hair.
Your tears fell from the ceiling on to my face.
I could not believe that when you came to die
Your breasts would die too and go underground.
Your nakedness, mirrored in the windowpane,
Made of God our icon and our peeping tom.

X-R A Y

I gaze at myself before I was born. A shadow
Against her liver and spine I share her body
With my brother's body, two skulls in a basket,
Two sets of bones that show no abnormalities.
I want her to eat the world, giblets, marrow,
Tripes and offal, fish, birds, fields of grain.
But because it is April nineteen thirty-nine
I should look up to the breasts that will weep for me
And prescribe in the dark a salad of landcress,
Fennel like hair, the sky-blue of borage flowers.

EVA BRAUN

The moon beams like Eva Braun's bare bottom
On rockets aimed at London, then at the sky
Where, in orbit to the dark side, astronauts
Read from *Mein Kampf* to a delighted world.

GEISHA

Though the partition opens at a touch
She makes a pin-hole and watches people
Watching the sky where a heavy bomber
Journeys to her mirror and jar of rouge.

BLITZ

They empty the swimming baths and lay out the dead.
There are children who haven't learned to swim, bundled
With budgerigars and tabbies under the stairs.
Shockwaves are wrinkling the water that isn't there.

TEREZÍN

No room has ever been as silent as the room
Where hundreds of violins are hung in unison.

GHETTO

I

Because you will suffer soon and die, your choices
Are neither right nor wrong: a spoon will feed you,
A flannel keep you clean, a toothbrush bring you back
To your bathroom's view of chimney-pots and gardens.
With so little time for inventory or leavetaking,
You are packing now for the rest of your life
Photographs, medicines, a change of underwear, a book,
A candlestick, a loaf, sardines, needle and thread.
These are your heirlooms, perishables, worldly goods.
What you bring is the same as what you leave behind,
Your last belonging a list of your belongings.

II

As though it were against the law to sleep on pillows
They have filled a cathedral with confiscated feathers:
Silence irrefrangible, no room for angels' wings,
Tons of feathers suffocating cherubim and seraphim.

III

The little girl without a mother behaves like a mother
With her rag doll to whom she explains fear and anguish,
The meagreness of the bread ration, how to make it last,
How to get back to the doll's house and lift up the roof
And, before the flame-throwers and dynamiters destroy it,
How to rescue from their separate rooms love and sorrow,
Masterpieces the size of a postage stamp, small fortunes.

IV

From among the hundreds of thousands I can imagine one
Behind the barbed-wire fences as my train crosses Poland.
I see him for long enough to catch the sprinkle of snowflakes
On his hair and schoolbag, and then I am transported
Away from that world of broken hobby-horses and silent toys.
He turns into a little snowman and refuses to melt.

V

For street-singers in the marketplace, weavers, warp-makers,
Those who suffer in sewing-machine repair shops, excrement-
Removal workers, there are not enough root vegetables,
Beetroots, turnips, swedes, nor for the leather-stitchers
Who are boiling leather so that their children may eat;
Who are turning like a thick slice of potato-bread
This page, which is everything I know about potatoes,
My delivery of Irish Peace, Beauty of Hebron, Home
Guard, Arran Banners, Kerr's Pinks, resistant to eelworm,
Resignation, common scab, terror, frost, potato-blight.

VI

There will be performances in the waiting room, and time
To jump over a skipping rope, and time to adjust
As though for a dancing class the ribbons in your hair.
This string quartet is the most natural thing in the world.

VII

Fingers leave shadows on a violin, harmonics,
A blackbird fluttering between electrified fences.

VIII

Lessons were forbidden in that terrible school.
Punishable by death were reading and writing
And arithmetic, so that even the junior infants
Grew old and wise in lofts studying these subjects.
There were drawing lessons, and drawings of kitchens
And farms, farm animals, butterflies, mothers, fathers
Who survived in crayon until in pen and ink
They turned into guards at executions and funerals
Torturing and hanging even these stick figures.
There were drawings of barracks and latrines as well
And the only windows were the windows they drew.

THE CAIRN AT DOOAGHTRY

Children lie under the cairn, unhallowed souls
Whose playground should be the duach and the dunes.
No higher than little children walking on tiptoe
Past SS guards at the selections in Terezín,
The cairn has become a scree, the scree a landslide
And a raised beach the memorial to all of them.

ARGOS

There were other separations, and so many of them
That Argos the dog who waited twenty years for Odysseus
Has gone on waiting, still neglected on the manure-heap
At our front door, flea-ridden, more dead than alive
Who chased wild goats once, and roe-deer; the favourite,
A real thoroughbred, a marvel at picking up the scent,
Who even now is wagging his tail and drooping his ears
And struggling to get nearer to the voice he recognises
And dying in the attempt; until like Odysseus
We weep for Argos the dog, and for all those other dogs,
For the rounding-up of hamsters, the panic of white mice
And the deportation of one canary called Pepicek.

PONIES

I

Carved out of the darkness and far below
In the very last working, a stable
Where the pressure transforms into trees
Pit-props, rosettes into sunflowers,
Into grazing nosebags and the droppings
That smoulder among lumps of coal.

II

Like the fuzzy star her forelock covers,
A yarn about a townland somewhere –
Two fields and no more, in one of them
The convergence of three counties, and her
Standing up to the gaskins in foxgloves,
Agrimony, swaying meadowsweet.

STONE-IN-OXNEY

for George Newson

At a table which seems to take root in the lawn
We breakfast late to a single propeller's drone,
The ghost of a Spitfire over Stone-in-Oxney
Or a Stuka, its turning-circle that cloud-gap
Or wherever you point to show me a bird; its dive
Low as the ceiling-beams in Chapel Cottage.
We bump against pilots who hang out of the sky.
Someone's hand is overshadowing the place-names,
Tracking the migration of wheatears and blackcaps
Who cross the Channel and make their landfall here.
Let him spread his fingers on a broken wing, now
Reed warblers are singing at Wittersham Levels
And at Small Hythe and Peening Quarter nightingales.

IN MEMORY OF CHARLES DONNELLY

Killed in Spain, 27.2.37, aged 22

I

Minutes before a bullet hits you in the forehead
There is a lull in the machine-gun fire, time to pick
From the dust a bunch of olives, time to squeeze them,
To understand the groans and screams and big abstractions
By saying quietly 'Even the olives are bleeding'.

II

Buried among the roots of that olive tree, you are
Wood and fruit and the skylight its branches make
Through which to read as they accumulate for ever
The poems you go on not writing in the tree's shadow
As it circles the fallen olives and the olive-stones.

THE ICE-CREAM MAN

Rum and raisin, vanilla, butter-scotch, walnut, peach:
You would rhyme off the flavours. That was before
They murdered the ice-cream man on the Lisburn Road
And you bought carnations to lay outside his shop.
I named for you all the wild flowers of the Burren
I had seen in one day: thyme, valerian, loosestrife,
Meadowsweet, tway blade, crowfoot, ling, angelica,
Herb robert, marjoram, cow parsley, sundew, vetch,
Mountain avens, wood sage, ragged robin, stitchwort,
Yarrow, lady's bedstraw, bindweed, bog pimpernel.

TRADE WINDS

I

Through Molly Ward's and Mickey Taylor's Locks,
Through Edenderry, Aghalee and Cranagh
To Lough Neagh and back again went Perseverence
And Speedwell carrying turf, coal and cinders.

II

Was it an Armagh man who loaded the boat
With the names of apples for his girlfriend:
Strawberry Cheeks, Lily Fingers, Angel Bites,
Winter Glories, Black Annetts, Widows' Whelps?

III

For smoking at wakes and breaking on graves
Carrick men christened clay pipes in Pipe Lane
Keel Baltic, Swinyard Cutty, Punch Quelp,
Plain Home Rule, Dutch Straws, Bent Unique.

IV

Among the Portavogie prawn-fishermen
Which will be the ship of death: Trade Winds,
Guiding Starlight, Halcyon, Easter Morn,
Liberty, Faithful Promise, Sparkling Wave?

THE BUTCHERS

When he had made sure there were no survivors in his house
And that all the suitors were dead, heaped in blood and dust
Like fish that fishermen with fine-meshed nets have hauled
Up gasping for salt water, evaporating in the sunshine,
Odysseus, spattered with muck and like a lion dripping blood
From his chest and cheeks after devouring a farmer's bullock,
Ordered the disloyal housemaids to sponge down the armchairs
And tables, while Telemachos, the oxherd and the swineherd
Scraped the floor with shovels, and then between the portico
And the roundhouse stretched a hawser and hanged the women
So none touched the ground with her toes, like long-winged
    thrushes
Or doves trapped in a mist-net across the thicket where they
    roost,
Their heads bobbing in a row, their feet twitching but not for
    long,
And when they had dragged Melanthios's corpse into the
    haggard
And cut off his nose and ears and cock and balls, a dog's dinner,
Odysseus, seeing the need for whitewash and disinfectant,
Fumigated the house and the outhouses, so that Hermes
Like a clergyman might wave the supernatural baton
With which he resurrects or hypnotises those he chooses,
And waken and round up the suitors' souls, and the housemaids',
Like bats gibbering in the nooks of their mysterious cave
When out of the clusters that dangle from the rocky ceiling
One of them drops and squeaks, so their souls were bat-
    squeaks
As they flittered after Hermes, their deliverer, who led them
Along the clammy sheughs, then past the oceanic streams
And the white rock, the sun's gatepost in that dreamy region,
Until they came to a bog-meadow full of bog-asphodels
Where the residents are ghosts or images of the dead.

NOTES

Some words may require a gloss: *machair* (p. 1) is Irish and Scots Gaelic for a sandy plain found behind dunes and affording some pasturage; *duach* (pp. 2, 5, 9, 44), the Irish for sandbanks or dunes, means in my part of Mayo the same as *machair*; *hover* (pp. 5 and 6) is an otter's temporary resting place, *holt* its den; *bullaun* (p. 13) is a square or cylindrical block of stone into which a deep hole has been cut to make a roughly shaped stone basin; *duncher* (p. 33) is Belfast dialect for a flat cap; *sheugh* (p. 51) is a trench or ditch – from the Irish.

In differing proportions and with varying degrees of high-handedness but always, I hope, with reverence, I have in seven of these poems combined free translation from Homer's *Odyssey* with original lines. The relevant passages are about the homecoming of Odysseus (Book XIII); his description of the bed and bedroom he'd built for Penelope (Book XXIII); the sequence of delayed recognitions and complicated reunions with his old nurse Eurycleia (Book XIX), his mother Anticleia in Hades (Book XI), his father Laertes (Book XXIV), his dog Argos (Book XVII); and the slaughter of the suitors and the journey of their souls to the underworld (Books XXII and XXIV).